Pocket Edition 100

DINOSAUR SCIENCE

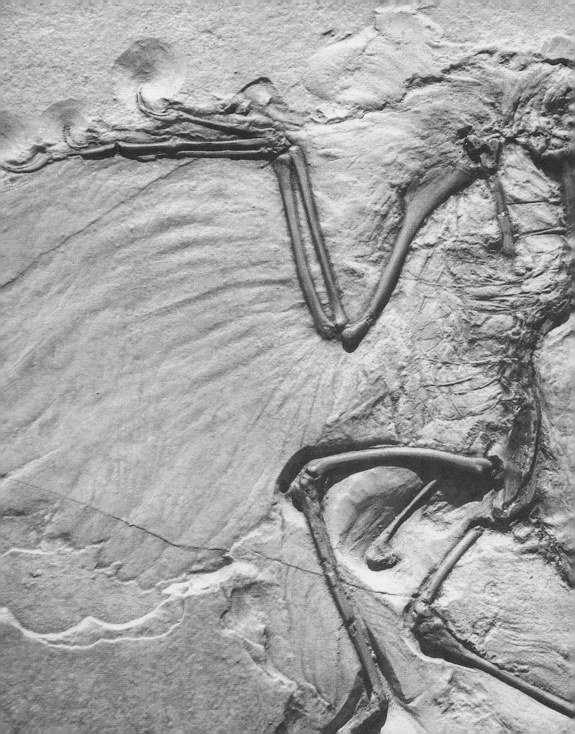

Pocket Edition

100 FACTS

DINOSAUR SCIENCE

Steve Parker

Consultant: John Malam

Miles Kelly

First published in 2017 by Miles Kelly Publishing Ltd, Harding's Barn, Bardfield End Green, Thaxted, Essex, CM6 3PX, UK

10 9 8 7 6 5 4 3 2 1

PUBLISHING DIRECTOR Belinda Gallagher
CREATIVE DIRECTOR Jo Cowan
EDITORIAL DIRECTOR Rosie Neave
DESIGN MANAGER Simon Lee
DESIGNER Andrea Slane
IMAGE MANAGER Liberty Newton
INDEXER Michelle Baker
PRODUCTION Elizabeth Collins, Caroline Kelly
REPROGRAPHICS Stephan Davis, Jennifer Cozens
ASSETS Lorraine King

ISBN 978-1-78617-612-7

Printed in China

British Library Cataloguing-in-Publication Data
A catalogue record for this book is available from the British Library

ACKNOWLEDGEMENTS
The publishers would like to thank the following artists who have contributed to this book:
Gabriel Alborozo, Peter Bull, Stuart Jackson-Carter

All other artwork from the Miles Kelly Artwork Bank

The publishers would like to thank the following sources for the use of their photographs:
Key: t = top, b = bottom, l = left, r = right, c = centre, m= main, bg = background, rt = used throughout
Cover (front) Science Picture Co/Science Photo Library
Alamy 9(bl) All Canada Photos; 10(cl) Artokoloro Quint Lox Limited; 15(cl) Carver Mostardi; 24(b) Q-Images; 27(br) Martin Shields; 30(bl) Lou-Foto; 33(cr) Nobumichi Tamura/Stocktrek Images; 35(cr) Martin Shields; 39(r) Reuters; 44–45(m) Mohamad Haghani
Ardea 18–19(m) Millard H. Sharp/Science Source
Diomedia 17(cl) Stocktrekimages RF/Rodolfo Nogueira; 22(t) Natural History Museum London UK; 26–27(t) Danita Delimont RM/Chuck Haney; 32–33(t) UIG Education; 46(m) Photos 12 Cinema/Archives du 7e Art/Universal Pictures
Getty 21(br) Karl Gehring; 24(cr) National Geographic; 32(bl) Bernard Weil
Nature Picture Library 11(c) Paul D Stewart
From DEVELOPMENTAL AND EVOLUTIONARY NOVELTY IN THE SERRATED TEETH OF THEROPOD DINOSAURS by Brink, K.S., Reisz, R.R., LeBlanc, A.R.H., Chang, R.S., Lee, Y.C., Chiang, C.C., Huang, T., and Evans, D.C., first published in Scientific Reports 5 in 2015, doi: 10.1038/srep12338 13(c)
Dr Gregory M. Erickson 13(bl)
From HOW BIG WAS 'BIG AL'? QUANTIFYING THE EFFECT OF SOFT TISSUE AND OSTEOLOGICAL UNKNOWNS ON MASS PREDICTIONS FOR ALLOSAURUS (DINOSAURIA:THEROPODA) by Karl T. Bates, Peter L. Falkingham, Brent H. Breithaupt, David Hodgetts, William I. Sellers, and Phillip L. Manning, first published in Palaeo Electronica in 2009, © Palaeontological Association 16(c)
Yale Peabody Museum 20(tr) Karen Ostrom
Polish Academy of Sciences, Institute of Paleobiology 22(c) and (bl)
From the permanent collection of The Judith River Foundation 36–37(m)
Dr Sarah Werning 40(tr and cr)
Dr Sergio Bertazzo 47
rspb.royalsocietypublishing 37(br) From MINERALIZED SOFT-TISSUE STRUCTURE AND CHEMISTRY IN A MUMMIFIED HADROSAUR FROM THE HELL CREEK FORMATION, NORTH DAKOTA (USA) by Phillip L. Manning, Peter M. Morris, Adam McMahon, Emrys Jones, Andy Gize, Joe H. S. Macquaker, George Wolff, Anu Thompson, Jim Marshall, Kevin G. Taylor, Tyler Lyson, Simon Gaskell, Onrapak Reamtong, William I. Sellers, Bart E. van Dongen, Mike Buckley, Roy A. Wogelius, first published in Proceedings of the Royal Society B on 1 July 2009.DOI: 10.1098/rspb.2009.0812
Shutterstock (rt) ESB Professional, donatas1205, donatas1205, Valentin Agapov, Kanate, happydancing, Jakub Krechowicz, somchaij; 10–11(rt) LiliGraphie; 10(tr) grintan; 14–15(bg) SignStudio; 16–17(bg) Stephen Rees; 17(tl) Michael Rosskothen, (tr) Linda Bucklin; 18–19(bg) Filipchuk Oleg; 25(br) Linda Bucklin; 35(tr) Catmando, (bl) Studio MARMILADE; 47 worldswildlifewonders
Science Photo Library 12(tl) Natural History Museum, London, (br) Paul D Stewart; 14(b) Claus Linau; 15(tr) Paul D Stewart, (br) Vincent Moncorge; 29(tr) British Antarctic Survey; 42(tr) Natural History Museum, London; 46(tl) Science Source

Every effort has been made to acknowledge the source and copyright holder of each picture.
Miles Kelly Publishing apologizes for any unintentional errors or omissions.

Made with paper from a sustainable forest

www.mileskelly.net

CONTENTS

Always new discoveries

1 **Every year, scientists discover around 15—20 new kinds of dinosaurs that became extinct (died out), millions of years ago.** These finds provide new information all the time. Just 50 years ago dinosaurs were thought to have been slow, scaly and stupid, but discoveries since then have revealed that dinosaurs did almost everything modern animals can do. Many dinosaurs had feathers and some could fly!

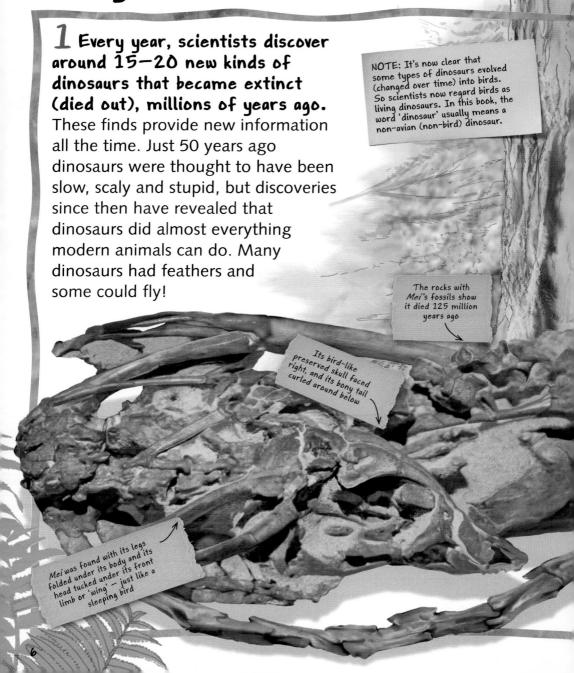

NOTE: It's now clear that some types of dinosaurs evolved (changed over time) into birds. So scientists now regard birds as living dinosaurs. In this book, the word 'dinosaur' usually means a non-avian (non-bird) dinosaur.

The rocks with *Mei*'s fossils show it died 125 million years ago

Its bird-like preserved skull faced right, and its bony tail curled around below

Mei was found with its legs folded under its body and its head tucked under its front limb or 'wing' — just like a sleeping bird

Mei could not fly; its feathers may have been for insulation

Mei was about 50 centimetres from snout-tip to tail-end

Mei's sharp claws held and ripped small prey

◀▲ Tiny *Mei* was among the most bird-like of the non-avian dinosaurs (see note). Discovered in China in 2004, its fossil remains showed it had feathers.

Secret lives of fossils

2 **We know about long-gone prehistoric animals from their fossils.** These usually formed when a dead body or its parts were slowly buried by small particles, like sand, ash or mud, and turned to stone over millions of years.

Ivan Efremov worked on fossils mainly in the Gobi Desert

3 **In 1940 Russian scientist Ivan Efremov (1908—1972) introduced the term 'taphonomy', meaning 'laws of burial'.** This is the study of when, how and why animals and plants form fossils, and the processes involved. Efremov's ideas were soon used by other fossil experts to understand what happened after animals and plants died.

Present day

Fossils are most visible in dry, windy places with little soil

1,000,000 years ago

10,000,000 years ago

Rocky minerals gradually replace the original bone minerals

WHO'S WHO?

Can you match the dinosaur species to the description of their fossil finds?

A. *Sinosauropteryx*
B. *Spinosaurus*

1. The biggest known meat-eater, adapted for swimming.
2. The first fossils found to show that dinosaurs had feathers.

Answers:
A = 2 B = 1

4 **Dinosaur fossils are usually of hard body parts like teeth, bones, horns and claws, and sometimes skin and scales.** Softer body parts like muscles and guts usually rot away, or get eaten by scavenging creatures, before they can be preserved.

5 **Fossils reveal more than the size and shape of the living dinosaur.** Cracks or gouges on bones suggest a scavenger. Fossils jumbled with rounded pebbles indicate the bones were washed along in water. If fossils are found in some kinds of sandstones it can mean the dinosaur lived in a dry habitat; other types of sandstones indicate a sandy riverbank. Fossils of other animals and plants help to recreate the dinosaur's habitat.

▼ A plant-eating *Protoceratops* and predatory *Velociraptor* fight to the death — an event that actually happened some 80 million years ago in the Gobi Desert, Mongolia. The two were preserved together as fossils, which were discovered in 1971.

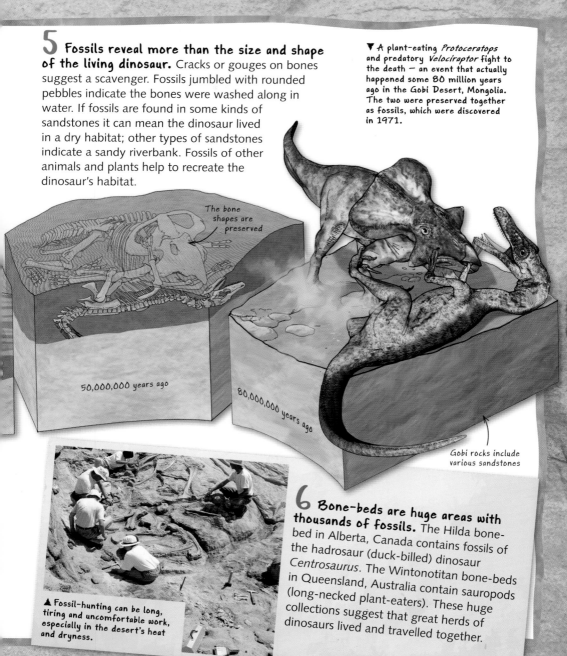

The bone shapes are preserved

50,000,000 years ago

80,000,000 years ago

Gobi rocks include various sandstones

▲ Fossil-hunting can be long, tiring and uncomfortable work, especially in the desert's heat and dryness.

6 **Bone-beds are huge areas with thousands of fossils.** The Hilda bone-bed in Alberta, Canada contains fossils of the hadrosaur (duck-billed) dinosaur *Centrosaurus*. The Wintonotitan bone-beds in Queensland, Australia contain sauropods (long-necked plant-eaters). These huge collections suggest that great herds of dinosaurs lived and travelled together.

Mega-discovery!

7 **The first scientific name was given to a dinosaur in 1824.** The main fossil was a piece of right lower jawbone with teeth from Stonesfield Quarry near Oxford, England. It was described by English churchman and fossil collector William Buckland (1784–1856), but both the identity of the finder and the date of discovery are unclear. It may have been dug up in 1797 or in 1815.

Robert Plot (1640–1696), whose *Natural History of Oxfordshire* (1676) contains the first known illustration of a dinosaur bone

8 **At Oxford, Buckland and colleagues examined the jawbone and other specimens.** From its sharp, similar-looking teeth in various stages of growth, they decided it was not a mammal, as mammals have teeth of different shapes, like canines and molars. Buckland said it was from a giant reptile 13 metres long. He named it *Megalosaurus*, meaning 'huge lizard'.

The original *Megalosaurus* jawbone drawing was in the journal *Transactions of the Geological Society*

1824

The first representations of *Megalosaurus* showed it as a massive lizard-like beast that plodded on all fours

1850s

Owen's
Megalosaurus

Owen's Iguanodon

9 In 1842 British fossil expert Richard Owen (1804–1892) named a new fossil reptile group Dinosauria — 'terrible' or 'awesome lizards'. He included three dinosaurs: *Megalosaurus*, *Iguanodon* and *Hylaeosaurus*. Owen pointed out many features of the skull, ribs, backbones, hips, limbs and feet that set dinosaurs apart from other reptiles. It is from Owen's work that we get the word 'dinosaur'.

Owen's
Hylaeosaurus

◀ Richard Owen became the first chief of the Natural History Museum in London, UK in 1881.

10 For years after, many fossils from big meat-eating dinosaurs were called *Megalosaurus*. The name became a 'wastebasket' for fossils that did not clearly belong to other kinds of dinosaurs.

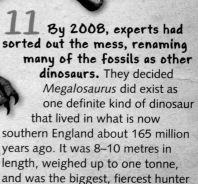

11 By 2008, experts had sorted out the mess, renaming many of the fossils as other dinosaurs. They decided *Megalosaurus* did exist as one definite kind of dinosaur that lived in what is now southern England about 165 million years ago. It was 8–10 metres in length, weighed up to one tonne, and was the biggest, fiercest hunter of its time.

Megalosaurus is now pictured running on its two big rear legs, like most meat-eating dinosaurs

Modern reconstruction

What teeth tell us

12 **The second dinosaur to receive an official scientific name was *Iguanodon* in 1825.** Gideon Mantell (1790–1852) started to study its first fossils – all teeth – in Sussex, in southern England, in 1821–1822. He recognized their distinctive shape was similar to, but much larger than, the teeth of the plant-eating iguana lizard.

◄ The tooth fossils of *Iguanodon* were apparently found in a pile of roadside rocks and stones, possibly by Mantell's wife Mary.

▼ Mantell announced the discovery of the fossil teeth, and the 'previously unknown reptile' they came from, in the science journal *Philosophical Transactions* of the Royal Society of London in January 1825.

Mantell was a country doctor and keen amateur geologist who spent much time studying rocks and landscapes

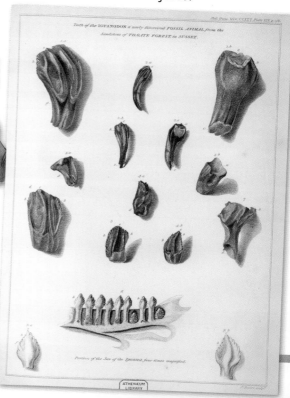

13 **Over the following years, other fossils were also described as *Iguanodon*.** Finds included up to 40 individuals found 320 metres deep in a Belgian coal mine in 1878. The Belgian mine fossils of *Iguanodon* differed from, and were much more complete than, those found by Gideon Mantell. So in 2007 Mantell's dinosaur was give a different name – *Mantellodon*.

14 **Teeth give many valuable clues to what a dinosaur ate.** For example, hadrosaurs or duckbills such as *Edmontosaurus* had rows of hundreds of broad, sharp-ridged cheek teeth, called 'dental batteries'. These were ideal for crushing and chewing tough vegetation such as twigs and conifer leaves.

Dental batteries

▲ The massed cheek teeth of a hadrosaur contrast with the toothless front or 'duck-billed' part of the mouth.

► Enlarging the teeth of the meat-eater *Gorgosaurus* shows the curved, chisel-edged serrations, which work more efficiently on flesh than triangular ones found on saw blades.

Individual serrations | Row of serrations | Whole tooth

15 **Most carnivorous or meat-eating dinosaurs had long, pointed teeth.** Those of the huge 13-metre-long *Carcharodontosaurus*, from Africa, were up to 20 centimetres long. They had serrated (jagged) edges for shearing and sawing through a victim. This hunter's name references the scientific name of the great white shark (*Carcharodon*), which has similar but smaller teeth.

▼ A laser scanner reveals the crests and hollows of the tooth grinding surfaces from the hadrosaur *Corythosaurus*. Each tooth is about the size of a baked bean.

2 mm

16 **Fossil teeth are examined with electron microscopes.** These see much smaller details than a light microscope. Marks called tooth microwear, as small as 1/100th of one millimetre in size, show what was eaten and how. Some hadrosaur teeth have many tiny, straight scrape marks at certain angles that show that as the dinosaur chewed, the outer surfaces of its lower teeth rubbed upwards and backwards against the inner surfaces of its upper teeth.

On the move

17 **Trace fossils are not remains of animals themselves, but signs and items they left behind.** These include footprints, tail drags, scratch marks, chewed food, eggshells, nests and burrows. Some of the most important dinosaur trace fossils are footprints. Lots in a row are known as trackways.

▲ A theropod (meat-eating) dinosaur left characteristic three-toed imprints, usually almost in a straight line.

18 **Dinosaur footprints can be preserved in several ways.** Often they are in soft sand or mud along a riverbank, lakeside or seashore. As they harden, they are then covered and protected by another layer of sand or mud, and so on. Some prints are made in the cooled ash that falls after a volcano erupts, which then hardens in the sun.

Fresh print made in soft mud

Mud hardens and bakes in the sun

Sand or similar particles fill the imprint

19 **Some of the first dinosaur footprints and tracks were described in the 1820s–30s.** Hundreds of them were found in Holyoke in Massachusetts, USA. The tracks were made 200 million years ago by dinosaurs that walked on two legs, probably small to medium meat-eaters. The dinosaurs are called *Eubrontes*. Bones, teeth or other parts have never been found, so *Eubrontes* is known only from its footprints.

▼ In the mid 19th century the Holyoke trackways became famous as a local curiosity.

20 **The footprint shape of a three-toed, long-clawed carnivore is very different to that of a round-footed sauropod.** The depth and spacing of prints indicate the animal's weight, leg length and how it was moving. Many prints together reveal a group of dinosaurs. Multiple tracks heading in one direction suggest travel – perhaps to a new feeding site.

One set of sauropod (plant-eating) dinosaur tracks had small prints in the middle and larger ones at the sides, suggesting adults were protecting youngsters in the middle

▲ A print from the carnivore *Dilophosaurus*, about 25 centimetres across, shows the large, pointed claw at each toe end.

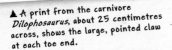

Soft rock is worn or eroded to leave footprint

▶ The largest sauropod prints measure up to one metre across, but their rounded shapes make it difficult to pinpoint the makers.

Smaller and bigger

21 **Measuring the bones of a fossil dinosaur skeleton can tell us the dinosaur's length, height and width.** But to estimate weight, a scale model of the dinosaur is put in water to find its volume. This is multiplied by the average density (weight per volume) of similar modern animals like crocodiles, lizards or birds.

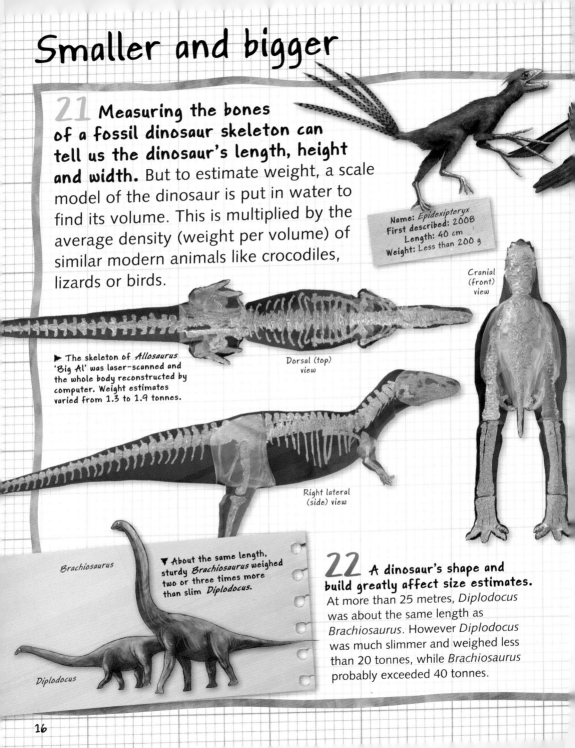

Name: *Epidexipteryx*
First described: 2008
Length: 40 cm
Weight: Less than 200 g

Cranial (front) view

▶ The skeleton of *Allosaurus* 'Big Al' was laser-scanned and the whole body reconstructed by computer. Weight estimates varied from 1.3 to 1.9 tonnes.

Dorsal (top) view

Right lateral (side) view

Brachiosaurus

▼ About the same length, sturdy *Brachiosaurus* weighed two or three times more than slim *Diplodocus*.

Diplodocus

22 **A dinosaur's shape and build greatly affect size estimates.** At more than 25 metres, *Diplodocus* was about the same length as *Brachiosaurus*. However *Diplodocus* was much slimmer and weighed less than 20 tonnes, while *Brachiosaurus* probably exceeded 40 tonnes.

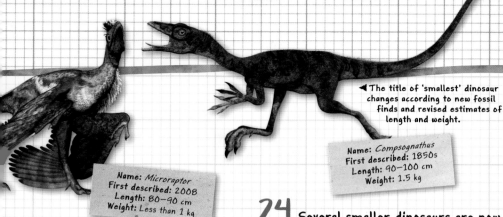

◄ The title of 'smallest' dinosaur changes according to new fossil finds and revised estimates of length and weight.

Name: *Compsognathus*
First described: 1850s
Length: 90–100 cm
Weight: 1.5 kg

Name: *Microraptor*
First described: 2008
Length: 80–90 cm
Weight: Less than 1 kg

24 **Several smaller dinosaurs are now known, including *Mei* and *Microraptor*.** *Parvicursor*, from 75 million years ago in Mongolia, was just 40 centimetres long and weighed less than 200 grams. *Epidexipteryx*, from northern China 165 million years ago, was perhaps slightly longer and about the same weight.

23 **For more than a century the smallest known dinosaur was *Compsognathus*.** Named in 1859, it lived in Europe about 150 million years ago, and was about 90–100 centimetres long and 1500 grams in weight.

BIGGEST-YET DINOSAUR
Fossils found: 2014
Length: More than 30 m
Weight: 70 tonnes

Name: *Giraffatitan*
First described: 1998
Length: 21–22 m
Weight: 40–50 tonnes

◄ 'Biggest' dinosaur usually means weight or mass, rather than length or height.

25 **For years the biggest dinosaur well known from fossils was *Giraffatitan*.** First described in 1914 as an African form of North American *Brachiosaurus*, it was given its own name in 1998. More huge dinosaur fossils are known but there are usually just a few, such as one or two backbones, so the dinosaur's size cannot be accurately estimated.

26 **In 2014, a new huge sauropod from 100 million years ago was found in Patagonia, South America.** With about 150 fossil bones from several individuals, it has been accurately sized. This vast animal was more than 30 metres long and 70 tonnes in weight.

Single or social?

27 **In 1947 a huge number of fairly small fossil dinosaurs was found at Ghost Ranch in New Mexico, USA.** They were identified as *Coelophysis* – a dinosaur about 3 metres long that lived 200 million years ago. It belonged to the theropod group – carnivores that ranged in size from tiny to huge and walked on two back legs.

The evidence

③

④

Coelophysis had been named in 1887 by the great dinosaur expert Edward Drinker Cope (1840–1897). He and his rival Othniel Charles Marsh found about 130 new kinds of dinosaurs between 1877 and 1897

▶ The Ghost Ranch fossils of *Coelophysis* were numerous, disjointed and jumbled up like a complicated 3D jigsaw puzzle.

Robust (probably male) form

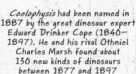

▶ Studies of dozens of *Coelophysis* skeletons revealed two 'average' forms.

Gracile (probably female) form

28 **The Ghost Ranch finds included two kinds of *Coelophysis*.** The 'robust' (sturdier, heavier) build would have weighed about 20 kilograms in life; the 'gracile' (slimmer, lighter) build about 15 kilograms. These were probably males and females, showing that, like many other animals, *Coelophysis* had differences between female and male individuals.

FIND OUT

Find out if the female or male is bigger on average in these animals:

1. Gorilla
2. Nile crocodile
3. *T. rex*
4. Peregrine falcon
5. Great white shark
6. Royal (ball) python
7. Human

KEY

1. Skull facing left
2. Neck and shoulder
3. Base of tail
4. Hip area
5. Main backbone

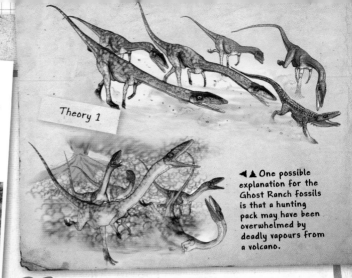

Theory 1

◀▲ One possible explanation for the Ghost Ranch fossils is that a hunting pack may have been overwhelmed by deadly vapours from a volcano.

29 The great numbers of fossils — probably more than 1000 individuals — led to new ideas about dinosaur behaviour. One idea was that *Coelophysis* roamed in a big pack, snapping up small prey, and that this group had all died together in some catastrophe, such as a volcanic eruption of poisonous fumes. Another theory was that the individuals had died in separate places and their bones were washed into one place by a flood.

30 More studies of the fossils' taphonomy suggest *Coelophysis* individuals gathered in groups around a pool in a valley. Perhaps they lived solitary lives but met at a waterhole during a drought and fell victim to a flash flood which washed their bones together.

Theory 2

▼ A second idea is that a sudden flood drowned separate dinosaurs and carried their various bones into one resting place.

Changing views

Ostrom did most of his fossil-digging in Wyoming, in midwest USA.

31 For over 100 years after their discovery, dinosaurs were seen as lumbering and rather stupid (lacking complicated behaviour). However in the 1960s, studies of *Deinonychus* by US fossil expert John Ostrom (1928–2005) changed many of these old ideas.

I DON'T BELIEVE IT!

Rods of bone along its tail bones meant *Deinonychus* could not bend its tail. It may have acted like a boat's rudder, swinging to one side to turn the dinosaur to the other side.

▶ One fossil find shows several *Deinonychus* in the same area as one plant-eater, the 8-metre-long *Tenontosaurus*. Maybe the meat-eaters were an attacking pack?

32 *Deinonychus* was a meat-eater in the dromaeosaur or 'raptor' group. It lived around 110 million years ago in North America, grew to around 3.5 metres in length, and weighed in at 70–100 kilograms. It had strong arms and hands and sharp finger claws. The extra-large, curved claw on the second toe of each foot could be flicked around to slash enemies and prey or hold them down.

Tenontosaurus whipped its tail around in self defence

33 In 1964 in Montana, USA, Ostrom and his team discovered more than 1000 bones and bone pieces from several *Deinonychus*. Ostrom examined details of the teeth, skeleton, shape of the skull and brain chamber inside, marks where the muscle joined the bones, and even micro-details inside the bones. The work took several years. In 1969 and 1974 he wrote reports on his findings.

Deinonychus dug in claws and teeth

34 The results showed that *Deinonychus* was much more similar to a warm-blooded bird than a cold-blooded reptile. It was fast, strong, agile and active. Its large brain might have made it quite intelligent. It may even have been warm-blooded.

Attacker biting vulnerable throat

▼ US expert Robert Bakker has continued and widened Ostrom's 'clever dinosaur' views.

35 Ostrom's work began the 'Dinosaur Renaissance'. Experts have since found more evidence that dinosaurs of many shapes and sizes were quick and clever, with bird-like behaviour. Further discoveries such as nests, feathers, and stages of evolution from dinosaurs into birds, have strengthened this thinking.

Built for speed?

36 **In 1965 huge shoulder, arm and hand bones with big claws were found in the Nemegt region of Mongolia.** They were discovered, along with a few other parts, by Polish expert Zofia Kielan-Jaworowska (1925–2015). In 1970 Polish expert Halszka Osmólska (1930–2008) and her colleagues named the dinosaur *Deinocheirus*, 'terrible' or 'horrible hand'.

◀ The original fossil hands and arms of *Deinocheirus*, with each toe and claw the size of a human arm and hand.

▼ The 1965 Polish expedition that discovered *Deinocheirus* was led by Zofia Kielan-Jaworowska. Her team was mostly female, which was very unusual for the time.

▼ Osmólska (left) led several expeditions to the Gobi Desert. Her teams included a number of Mongolian and Chinese workers.

37 **The identity of *Deinocheirus* remained a mystery for decades.** Then in 2012, experts announced more fossils, including ribs, found at the original dig site in Mongolia. Some had bite marks, indicating *Deinocheirus* had been attacked or scavenged by *Tarbosaurus*, the Asian cousin of *Tyrannosaurus*.

38 By 2013, further finds showed *Deinocheirus* was actually a massive ornithomimosaur (ostrich-dinosaur). Ornithomimosaurs were a specialized group of meat-eating theropods. At 11 metres and 6 tonnes, *Deinocheirus* was as big as *Tyrannosaurus*. It had a tall back hump or sail, possibly fan-like tail feathers, and weak jaws with small teeth suited to soft plant food.

▼ At more than 4 metres tall, *Deinocheirus* was by far the largest of the ornithomimosaurs, or 'ostrich mimics'.

Deinocheirus
Length: 11 m

39 *Deinocheirus* lived 70 million years ago and was a huge and unusual ornithomimosaur. Most of its group were much smaller. They were slim and lightweight, with long necks and arms, and very long, powerful back legs – similar to the ostrich bird. They include the 4.5-metre *Struthiomimus* and 3.7-metre *Ornithomimus*. Some had feathers and they were the fastest of all dinosaurs, running perhaps at 70–80 kilometres per hour.

▶▼ Ostrich-dinosaurs had large, powerful rear legs, but also sizeable arms, hands and claws, perhaps for scrabbling in soil and undergrowth for food.

Ornithomimus
Length: 3.7 m

Struthiomimus
Length: 4.5 m

40 The *Deinocheirus* fossils had a complicated history. Some were stolen from dig sites in Mongolia, sold in secret and sent abroad without permits to collectors, and even broken into pieces and sold again to make more money. It took several years to track them down and return them to Mongolia.

Scythe-claws

41 In 1973, a number of strange fossils were uncovered in Mongolia, Asia. They looked like dinosaur remains but they had some puzzling features, such as a slim jawbone with peg-like teeth and a thickset, sturdy thighbone that did not seem to belong together. In 1979 they were named as *Segnosaurus*, meaning 'slow lizard'.

```
          SAURISCHIA
          Lizard-hipped
           dinosaurs

  SAUROPODS                          THEROPODS
  Long-necked,                       All meat-
  long-tailed      SEGNOSAURS         eaters
  plant-eaters
```

▲ When first studied, therizinosaurs were called segnosaurs and viewed as a main group of saurischians.

▼ Therizinosaur teeth are small, numerous and best suited to chopping soft vegetation.

I DON'T BELIEVE IT!

At first, the huge claws of *Therizinosaurus* were believed to come from a huge turtle, which used them to rake up and slice off seaweed to eat.

42 More, similar finds turned up in the same region over the following years, including some very long finger claws. Experts began to link these to several curved, sword-like claws, almost one metre long, that had been found in Mongolia in 1948, and named by Russian fossil expert Evgeny Maleev (1915–1966) as *Therizinosaurus* in 1954.

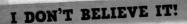

▼ The original therizinosaur fossil claw measures 56 cm in length. Others found since are even longer.

SAURISCHIA
Lizard-hipped
dinosaurs

SAUROPODS
Long-necked, long-tailed
plant-eaters

THEROPODS
All meat-eaters

▲ Newer theories place
plant-eating therizinosaurs
as a subgroup of otherwise
meat-eating theropods.

THERIZINOSAURS

▶ *Therizinosaurus* was a
massive creature with very
low, wide hips unsuited for
fast movement.

43 **In the 1990s–2000s more finds in China and elsewhere in Asia helped to solve the puzzle.** The new group of dinosaurs were named therizinosaurs, 'scythe' or 'reaper lizards', based on the long claws. Most lived around 130 to 70 million years ago in Asia, with a few in North America.

44 **Therizinosaurs were a surprise.** They walked on two back legs and had complex wrist joints, placing them in the theropod (carnivore) group. Yet their small, sharp, curved teeth indicate a diet of plants. And some were huge – at 10 metres long and 5 tonnes in weight *Therizinosaurus* was almost as big as *Tyrannosaurus*.

▼ *Beipiaosaurus* lived about 125 million years ago in what is now north-east China.

45 ***Beipiaosaurus* was one of the first therizinosaurs.** Well known from plentiful fossils, it was 2.3 metres long with a stocky body, typical long finger claws, wide hips, and short tail bones like a bird's. It was almost entirely covered in feathers.

◀ *Falcarius*, about 4 metres long, was a North American therizinosaur.

25

Caring parents

46 From 1977–1978, thousands of fossils near Choteau in Montana, USA revealed exciting new facts about dinosaur reproduction. There were so many fossil eggs, in particular, that the site became known as 'Egg Mountain'.

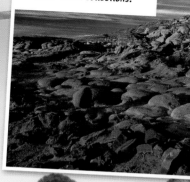

▼ 'Egg Mountain' is part of the Rocky Mountains and one of the world's largest dinosaur fossil collections.

47 Egg Mountain was a huge collection of *Maiasaura* nests — similar to a seabird breeding colony. *Maiasaura* was a plant-eating hadrosaur (duck-billed dinosaur) that grew to about 9 metres long and lived 77 million years ago. Its name means 'good earth mother'.

▼ The nests were bowl shapes about one metre across scooped in the earth. They were 7–8 metres apart, so an adult on one nest could not reach its neighbours.

Tiny embryo is nourished by yolk

Developing embryo

Fully formed baby fills the space inside egg

Hatchling

QUIZ

Can you put the following dinosaur breeding activities in the right order?

A. Scrape a nest bowl in the soil.

B. Cover eggs with rotten vegetation to keep them warm and protected.

C. Guard and feed the babies until they can run well.

D. Lay eggs in the nest.

Answer:
A D B C

48 Each *Maiasaura* nest contained 30–40 eggs about 15–20 centimetres in length, arranged in a spiral. Plant remains indicate that the adults probably covered the eggs with rotting vegetation for warmth, as some birds do today. Fossils of newly hatched babies show teeth worn from eating, yet their leg bones were not strong enough for walking. Adults probably brought food to the nests, showing parental care – like many birds but few reptiles.

49 The fossils were examined by US experts John (known as 'Jack') Horner (1946–) and Robert Makela (1940–1987). Their work revealed dinosaurs to be far more bird-like than previously thought. Horner later worked as an advisor on the *Jurassic Park* movie series.

← 'Jack' Horner has made many advances in our knowledge of how dinosaurs grew and developed

50 There are also fossils of growing *Maiasaura* babies that show how they developed. Within a year they increased from 30–40 centimetres in length to 1.5 metres, which is a growth rate similar to some birds. As well as *Maiasaura*, fossils of the 2.5-metre plant-eater *Orodromeus* and the skeletons and eggs of the similar-sized, slim, fast meat-eater *Troodon* were also found at Egg Mountain.

▼ Many fossil dinosaur embryos have since been found, such as this oviraptosaur.

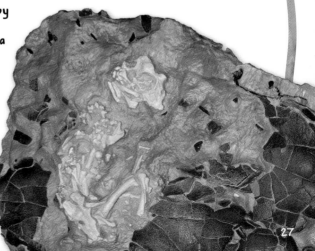

Frozen fossils

51 **Long ago, Antarctica's climate, and the whole world, were much warmer.** We know this from the fossils found there, plus evidence from continental drift (the gradual movement of the continental landmasses across the Earth's surface over time). There were trees and other plants, and a wide variety of animals.

▶ *Cryolophosaurus* had a curious bony snout crest that resembled a seashell or decorative comb.

53 **Dinosaur fossils have also been found in the far north, in the Arctic.** They include various kinds of ceratopsians (horned dinosaurs), and 9-metre-long hadrosaurs or duck-bills such as *Edmontosaurus*.

▼ About 140 million years ago the land masses of former southern supercontinent Gondwana began to split apart, as Antarctica and Australia drifted southwards.

Early Cretaceous Period

Late Cretaceous Period

52 **In 1986 the first dinosaur fossils were found in the far south of the world, on James Ross Island in Antarctica.** The remains were from a 4-metre-long ankylosaur (armoured dinosaur) that lived 70 million years ago, named *Antarctopelta* in 2006. Several more dinosaur remains have since been discovered, including the 6-metre, half-tonne carnivore *Cryolophosaurus* from 190 million years ago.

► Fossil digs in polar regions, like this one here on Seymour Island, Antarctica, have only a very short season of suitable conditions.

▲ Polar dinosaurs may have made long migrations to find food and warmth.

54 **With today's position and climate, excavating fossils in places like Antarctica and the Arctic is very difficult.** It is too cold and dark for much of the year to stay there. It is also very remote, so food, equipment and heavy fossils must be transported long distances, often by helicopter, which is very costly.

Present day

FIND THE FOSSIL

Dinosaur fossils have been found on every continent. Can you find out where the fossils of these dinosaurs were found?

1. Spinosaurus
2. Leaellynasaura
3. Iguanodon
4. Herrerasaurus
5. Therizinosaurus
6. Diplodocus

55 *Leaellynasaura* **was a small plant-eater, about one metre long.** It lived 115 million years ago in southern Australia, which was then linked to Antarctica. It had large eyes, perhaps to see in the gloom during the far-south winter when the sun was low or did not even rise. Plant fossils indicate the growing season stopped for a time, so maybe *Leaellynasaura* had a long winter rest, or even hibernated.

▼ *Leaellynasaura* had very big eyes for its skull and body size, to see in dim light.

29

Details from Liaoning

Sinornithosaurus

56 **From the early 1990s, stunning fossil remains were found in China.** Hundreds of new dinosaurs have been discovered in the north-east province of Liaoning. These finds have changed thinking about dinosaur behaviours and their classification (grouping).

CHINA

CHINA

Liaoning Province

▲ Liaoning, perhaps the world's number one 'fossil hotspot', borders the Yellow Sea.

▼ *Sinornithosaurus* fossils, found in 1999, clearly showed feathers.

57 **The rocks of Liaoning belong to the Jehol Group, and range from 165—100 million years old.** The main dinosaur fossils are from the Early Cretaceous Period, about 130 to 115 million years ago.

▼ Around 125–120 million years ago Liaoning's volcanic habitat supported a diverse range of plant and animal life.

Caudipteryx

Dilong

Liaoningosaurus

Psittacosaurus

59 *Liaoningosaurus* **was named after Liaoning in 2001.** This beautifully preserved ankylosaur (armoured dinosaur), was 35 centimetres long, although it was a youngster so adults would be several times larger. Other examples of dinosaur fossils found in the area include *Mei, Dilong, Psittacosaurus, Microraptor, Beipiaosaurus, Sinosauropteryx, Caudipteryx* and *Sinornithosaurus*.

58 **At that time numerous volcanoes erupted frequently.** They sent out deadly fumes and very fine ash, which quickly killed nearby living things, and covered them before they could decay. The ash particles kept many details, such as skin, scales, feathers, and even signs of inner parts, intact.

60 **Thousands of other bird fossils, as well as fossils of non-dinosaur animals, were also found at Liaoning.** These include insects, fish, turtles and mammals. Plant fossils have also been discovered. All this allows detailed reconstruction of whole habitats during the Early Cretaceous.

31

Feathered friends

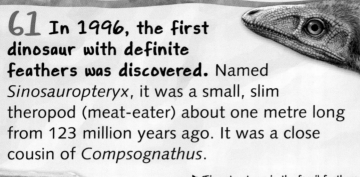

61 **In 1996, the first dinosaur with definite feathers was discovered.** Named *Sinosauropteryx*, it was a small, slim theropod (meat-eater) about one metre long from 123 million years ago. It was a close cousin of *Compsognathus*.

▶ Tiny structures in the fossil feathers of *Sinosauropteryx* suggest it was shades of dark and light brown, with a banded or ringed tail.

▼ Feathers are clearly visible in this fossil of *Sinosauropteryx*, especially along the dorsal or upper neck and back.

'Fuzz' of dorsal feathers

62 **The fossils of *Sinosauropteryx*, ('Chinese reptile wing'), came from Liaoning, China.** The feathers were too small and the wrong design for flight. They were more like filaments (strands) or a bird's down feathers. The length of feathers varied from 15 millimetres on the head to 40 millimetres on the hips and tail.

TRUE OR FALSE?

1. *Yutyrannus* was 12 metres long.
2. The name *Sinosauropteryx* means 'Chinese bird wing'.
3. *Caudipteryx's* tail feathers were larger than its body feathers.
4. *Kulindadromeus* lived in what is now Romania.

Answers:
1. False, it was 9 metres long
2. False, it means 'Chinese reptile wing'
3. True 4. False – it lived in what is now Russia

63 Other dinosaurs have been found with similar strand- or down-like feathers.

These include the turkey-sized theropod *Caudipteryx*, which also had a tail fan of larger feathers, and the fearsome 9-metre-long theropod *Yutyrannus*. Downy feathers may have been for insulation. Or they might have been for visual display – with bright colours to attract mates, as in many birds.

▲ *Yutyrannus* is the largest dinosaur with direct fossil evidence of feathers.

Caudipteryx had feathery fans on its arms and tail

65 The first herbivorous (non-theropod) dinosaur fossils to show a feather-like covering were of *Kulindadromeus*.

Named in 2014, it was 1.5 metres long, lived 160–150 million years ago in Russia, and was only distantly related to theropods. Its discovery suggests that many kinds of dinosaurs had feathers, but in most cases the feathers were not preserved.

64 Feathers are thought to have first evolved as simple hair-like strands, probably from reptile scales.

Some developed side branches at the base to form multi-strand plumes. In others, side branches evolved from a central shaft, eventually developing into true flight feathers.

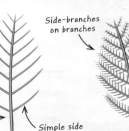

◀ *Kulindadromeus* had three types of feathers, showing their evolution was well under way in the Jurassic Period.

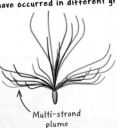

▼ Tracing the path of feather development is tricky, because the changes seem to have occurred in different groups at various times.

Simple strand or filament

Multi-strand plume

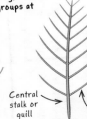
Central stalk or quill

Simple side branches

Side-branches on branches

Taking to the skies

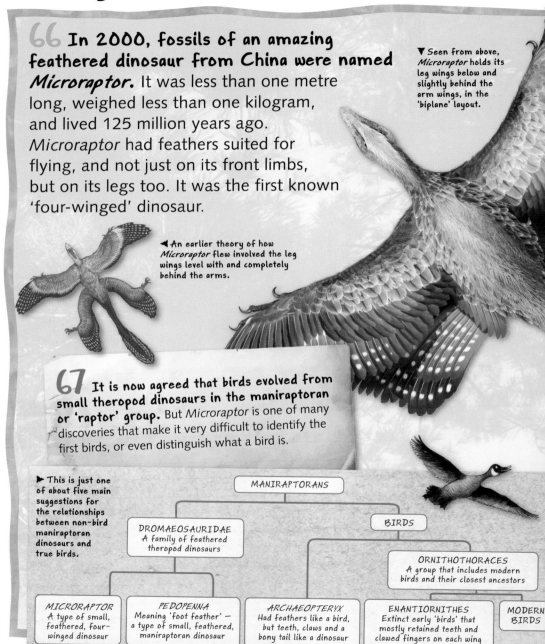

66 **In 2000, fossils of an amazing feathered dinosaur from China were named *Microraptor*.** It was less than one metre long, weighed less than one kilogram, and lived 125 million years ago. *Microraptor* had feathers suited for flying, and not just on its front limbs, but on its legs too. It was the first known 'four-winged' dinosaur.

▼ Seen from above, *Microraptor* holds its leg wings below and slightly behind the arm wings, in the 'biplane' layout.

◄ An earlier theory of how *Microraptor* flew involved the leg wings level with and completely behind the arms.

67 **It is now agreed that birds evolved from small theropod dinosaurs in the maniraptoran or 'raptor' group.** But *Microraptor* is one of many discoveries that make it very difficult to identify the first birds, or even distinguish what a bird is.

► This is just one of about five main suggestions for the relationships between non-bird maniraptoran dinosaurs and true birds.

MANIRAPTORANS

DROMAEOSAURIDAE
A family of feathered theropod dinosaurs

BIRDS

ORNITHOTHORACES
A group that includes modern birds and their closest ancestors

MICRORAPTOR
A type of small, feathered, four-winged dinosaur

PEDOPENNA
Meaning 'foot feather' — a type of small, feathered, maniraptoran dinosaur

ARCHAEOPTERYX
Had feathers like a bird, but teeth, claws and a bony tail like a dinosaur

ENANTIORNITHES
Extinct early 'birds' that mostly retained teeth and clawed fingers on each wing

MODERN BIRDS

▲ *Archaeopteryx* had a wingspan of about 50 centimetres and was probably an able, but not expert, flier.

68 **Recent finds have changed our view of** *Archaeopteryx.* Named in 1861 and long regarded as the first bird, it lived in Europe 150 million years ago. Several earlier birds are now known, such as *Aurornis* ('dawn bird'), from 160 million years ago in China.

▶ The fossils of *Anchiornis* show it was about 40 centimetres in length but weighed less than one quarter of a kilogram.

69 *Anchiornis,* ('near bird') lived **160 million years ago in China.** Discovered in 2009, its full name is *Anchiornis huxleyi*, honouring English biologist Thomas Henry Huxley (1825–1895). An early supporter of the theory of evolution, he was among the first to suggest birds evolved from dinosaurs. His ideas were ignored for 130 years but are now accepted.

70 **The features that separate birds from their non-bird dinosaur cousins are much debated.** As well as feathers and flapping flight, they often involve certain features of the skeleton, such as the shoulder, arm and wrist bones. As more discoveries are made, these differences may well change yet again.

◀ The variable hawk is one of some 10,000 species of living birds.

Mummified!

71 **Most dinosaur fossils are of hard body parts, but 'Leonardo' was different.** Discovered in 2000 in Montana, USA, its fossilized remains included scales, skin, muscles, guts, heart and liver. Leonardo is known as a 'dinosaur mummy', because its preservation was a natural version of how people preserved ancient Egyptian pharaohs.

KEY

1. Backbones
2. Tendons along backbones
3. Neck
4. Lungs
5. Heart
6. Stomach
7. Liver
8. Intestines

72 **Leonardo was a *Brachylophosaurus* hadrosaur (duckbill) that lived 77 million years ago.** It grew to 10 metres long and 7 tonnes in weight when adult, but Leonardo was smaller, only about four years old when it died.

► As well as chewed leaves, Leonardo's guts contained seeds and pollen from over 40 different plants.

73 **Cutting Leonardo open would have destroyed the fossil.** Instead it was taken to Houston Space Center in Texas, USA, and studied with high-energy X-ray scanners and similar methods to produce images of its insides. These showed signs of a bag-like crop, as in birds, to store just-eaten food. In the stomach were chewed pieces of plants including ferns, conifers and magnolias, plus worm parasites.

Rear legs

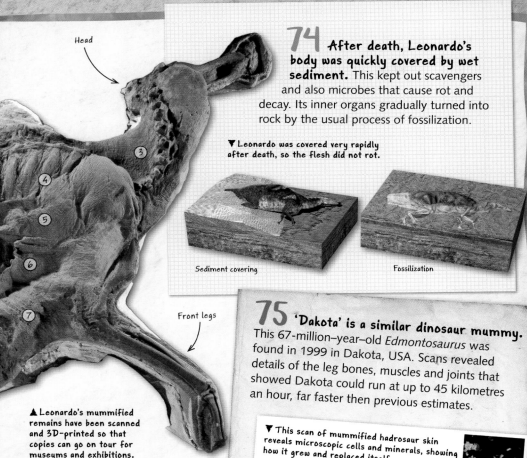

Head

3

4

5

6

7

Front legs

74 **After death, Leonardo's body was quickly covered by wet sediment.** This kept out scavengers and also microbes that cause rot and decay. Its inner organs gradually turned into rock by the usual process of fossilization.

▼ Leonardo was covered very rapidly after death, so the flesh did not rot.

Sediment covering

Fossilization

▲ Leonardo's mummified remains have been scanned and 3D-printed so that copies can go on tour for museums and exhibitions.

75 **'Dakota' is a similar dinosaur mummy.** This 67-million-year-old *Edmontosaurus* was found in 1999 in Dakota, USA. Scans revealed details of the leg bones, muscles and joints that showed Dakota could run at up to 45 kilometres an hour, far faster then previous estimates.

▼ This scan of mummified hadrosaur skin reveals microscopic cells and minerals, showing how it grew and replaced itself.

I DON'T BELIEVE IT!

The fossil-hunters who found Leonardo named it after some writing scrawled over 100 years ago on the rocks nearby: 'Leonard Webb loves Geneva Jordan 1916.'

Egg thief?

SORT BY SIZE

Look for information in books and online that will help you put these oviraptosaurs in size order. Some of the clues are on this page and some are in their names.

Gigantoraptor, Citipati, Microraptor, Oviraptor, Conchoraptor ('conch' means 'snail')

76 **In 2001 a dinosaur discovery from Mongolia was named *Citipati*, which means 'lord of the funeral pyre'.** It lived about 80 million years ago and stood as tall as a human.

77 ***Citipati* was in the group called oviraptosaurs.** These were theropods that walked on their two back legs and had powerful, bird-like beaked mouths. The first member discovered was *Oviraptor* way back in 1924, also in Mongolia. It was smaller than *Citipati*.

78 ***Oviraptor's* remains were next to a nest of dinosaur eggs — some of the first to be discovered.** Its name means 'egg thief' because at the time it was believed to be stealing the eggs of another dinosaur – perhaps the plant-eater *Protoceratops* – to crush with its strong beak and eat. But no more *Oviraptor* fossils came to light and it remained a puzzle.

▼ At first, the fossil finds were interpreted as a speedy *Oviraptor* making a raid on the nest of a plant-eater when it died.

Old theory

79 In the 1990s more *Citipati* fossils were found, many also near eggs. The use of X-rays and other methods showed developing oviraptosaur babies inside the eggs, not *Protoceratops*. Scientists decided *Citipati* was not stealing eggs, but protecting its own nest. Canadian fossil expert Philip Currie (1949–) and colleagues suggested the original *Oviraptor* was also on its own nest. Further finds showed this to be correct.

◄ While incubating its eggs, *Citipati* would have had to watch out for potential egg-stealing intruders.

▼ It is now thought to be more likely that *Oviraptor* was protecting its own nest and keeping its own eggs warm.

New theory

▲ Information from this *Saltasaurus* embryo CT scan can be adapted and combined with other sauropod discoveries.

80 'Borrowing' information from one dinosaur to fill in missing information about another is common. Many famous dinosaurs have parts never found as fossils, but instead adapted from close relations. For example, early versions of *Apatosaurus* used a skull from *Camarasaurus*.

Growing up

81 **Finding many fossils of the same dinosaur at different ages and sizes shows how — and how fast — it got bigger and reached adult size.** This is known as a 'growth series'. Growth patterns are known for dozens of dinosaurs, from giant sauropods to small raptors.

▲► In this cut-through shin bone from a young adult *Tenontosaurus*, fast-growing bone tissue is to the left.

82 **One dinosaur for which the growth series is known is the plant-eating ceratopsian (horn-faced) *Psittacosaurus*.** It lived 120–100 million years ago in East Asia, and was just 12 centimetres long and 0.3 kilograms in weight as a hatchling. By the time it reached 3 years old it was 2–3 kilograms, and at full size (7–8 years) it was 160 centimetres and 20 kilograms.

▲ In an older adult, the fast-growing tissue had mostly faded, with mature bone taking its place.

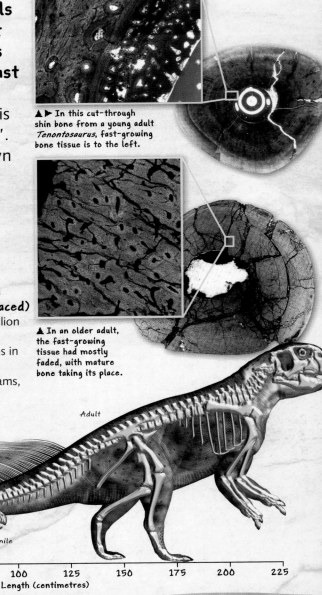

Adult

► *Psittacosaurus* increased 13 times in length and 60 times in weight from hatchling to adult.

Baby

Juvenile

0	25	50	75	100	125	150	175	200	225

Length (centimetres)

83 In 2003–4 studies of *Tyrannosaurus* fossil bones showed the speed and timing of its growth. The bones were measured in detail and their sizes plotted on graphs. Some bones were sliced, revealing growth rings – similar to those in tree trunks – that indicated yearly growth.

85 Different parts of a dinosaur's body grew at different rates. Like many other animals, body shape and proportions changed with age. For example, the neck frill and horns of a young *Triceratops* were much smaller in proportion to its head and body, compared to the adult. This is known as 'allometry' (different measures).

▼ The face horns of *Triceratops* were small lumps at first, but grew faster than the rest of the skull.

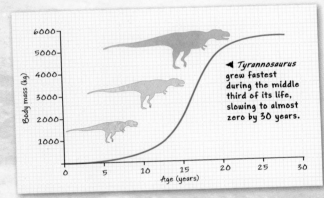

◄ *Tyrannosaurus* grew fastest during the middle third of its life, slowing to almost zero by 30 years.

Body mass (kg)

6000
5000
4000
3000
2000
1000

0   5   10   15   20   25   30
Age (years)

Baby

Small juvenile

Large juvenile

Adult

84 The results showed *Tyrannosaurus* was less than one metre long and weighed just a few kilograms in its first year. It grew fairly slowly until 12–13 years of age. Then it had a teenage growth spurt when it put on up to 2 kilograms per day! By 20 years, growth slowed. Full adult size was reached around age 25.

I DON'T BELIEVE IT!

Like many other young animals, baby dinosaurs looked 'cute' because they had a relatively large head and small limbs.

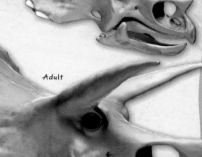

Mapping the brain

86 **In 2013, a study showed the first detailed view inside a dinosaur brain.** It was made using fossil skulls of dinosaurs such as *Tyrannosaurus* and the similar *Allosaurus* (a 10-metre-long predator from 150 million years ago), the early bird *Archaeopteryx*, and also the brains of living birds and alligators.

▶ A merged alligator-bird brain was 'remodelled' to fit the space inside the skull's cerebral cavity of *Tyrannosaurus*.

▲▼ Bird brains are much larger in proportion to their body size than alligators', but share many similarities.

87 **Alligators belong to the same major reptile group — archosaurs — as dinosaurs, and birds evolved from dinosaurs.** The study looked at the detailed shapes of alligator and bird brains and what the parts did in life. Then a computer 'reshaped' a combined alligator-bird brain to fit inside a dinosaur skull.

88 **A well-preserved dinosaur skull has hollows or chambers inside.** Some were airways, others were for nerves and blood vessels. The brain was in a larger chamber at the skull's upper rear. Sometimes this chamber filled during fossilization, forming a rocky lump shaped like the original brain, known as an endocast.

▶ An *Iguanodon* endocast includes main nerves and vessels going to and from the brain.

89 **Results showed the brains of dinosaurs like *Tyrannosaurus* had well developed parts for sight, smell, hearing and coordination.** Also developed were parts for complex behaviour, learning and vocalization (making sounds).

Maybe *Tyrannosaurus* made soft calls to its mate, as well as loud noises to frighten enemies, much like living alligators and birds

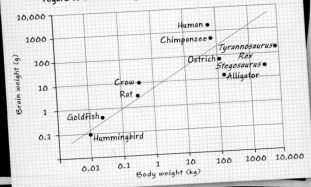

▼ A chart comparing brain and body sizes puts what we regard as more 'intelligent' animals above the red line.

Brain weight (g)

10,000						Human •	
1000					Chimpanzee •		Tyrannosaurus • Rex
100					Ostrich •	Stegosaurus •	
						• Alligator	
10			Crow •				
			Rat •				
1	Goldfish •						
0.1	• Hummingbird						

0.01   0.1   1   10   100   1000   10,000
Body weight (kg)

First swimmer

90 In 2014, a report on *Spinosaurus* said it was a semiaquatic dinosaur. This means it was adapted for life in water as well as on land. *Spinosaurus* had previously been thought to be the largest-ever land carnivore. The experts who compiled the report included US fossil-hunter Paul Sereno (1957–), whose other famous fossil discoveries include the giant crocodile *Sarcosuchus* and the huge carnivorous dinosaur *Carcharodontosaurus*.

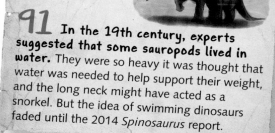

It was once thought that sauropods waded in lakes, feeding on water plants

91 In the 19th century, experts suggested that some sauropods lived in water. They were so heavy it was thought that water was needed to help support their weight, and the long neck might have acted as a snorkel. But the idea of swimming dinosaurs faded until the 2014 *Spinosaurus* report.

92 The front of *Spinosaurus*'s body was adapted for swimming and hunting. These included long slim jaws, interlocking teeth and large clawed fingers to grab slippery prey such as fish, as well as fleshy nostrils that could close underwater, and a long bendy neck.

▶ *Spinosaurus* pursues a sawfish, with kicking rear legs and swishing tail.

'Rosette' of long teeth at mouth front to grab victim

93 *Spinosaurus* also had a slim body, with small hips and back legs for streamlining. Its limb bones were solid and heavy to dive easily in water, not air-filled and light as in other dinosaurs, which would make diving difficult.

Spinosaurinae

Irritator

Spinosaurus

Spinosauridae

Ichthyovenator

Baryonychinae

Suchomimus

Baryonyx

▶ Recent discoveries show there were probably two main groups of spinosaurs, all large predators.

↑ Powerful leg muscles

Partially webbed back feet

94 The muscles that worked *Spinosaurus's* thighs would have produced a kicking action ideal for swimming. The flattened, partly webbed feet and toe claws worked like flippers, and the tail bones were loosely joined so the tail could swish to and fro like a crocodile's to push through water.

95 Other fossils from the area, North Africa, show *Spinosaurus* lived in a warm climate 100 million years ago. Plentiful rain, rivers and lakes meant fish, turtles and other water creatures were common. At more than 15 metres and weighing over 10 tonnes, *Spinosaurus* could overpower them all.

Genes and dreams

◀ The 2015 movie *Jurassic World* features a giant carnivore called *Indominus* — a hybrid created with DNA from various creatures.

96 **There have been several reports of dinosaur DNA (deoxyribonucleic acid) from fossils such as bones, teeth and eggs.** DNA is genetic material that contains the instructions for how a living thing develops, works and survives. So could this DNA be used to make living dinosaurs, like in the movies?

▲ The structure of DNA fragments is studied by a method called gel electrophoresis.

99 In 2015, partly preserved red blood cells and collagen (bone fibres) were detected in a dinosaur claw that was 75 million years old. This work used new techniques including ion beam stripping and advanced mass spectrometry.

97 **Tests showed that several reports of dinosaur DNA were false.** Some of it was proved to be from living animals that had touched the exposed fossils. Some was from people who excavated the fossils, or tested the samples. Others were too tiny and damaged to be useful.

98 **Even if some dinosaur DNA was found, it would probably be tiny, damaged pieces.** Using a few jumbled fragments from millions to make a living dinosaur would be impossible with current technology.

▲ Various cells shapes have been identified in fossil dinosaur tissues, including red blood cells.

◀ Recreating extinct dinosaurs would take vast effort and finance, which some argue is better spent on saving their living descendants — birds.

100 **So what of the future?** Amazing fossil finds around the world and developments in technology will probably continue to speed up. Experts from 30 years ago would hardly believe what we know now. It's hard to even imagine where dinosaur science will be 30 years from now.

Index